Crochet Granny Square Motifs and Joining Techniques Book
Elevate Your Crocheting Skills

Abu B Baldwin

Table of Contents

Thank you for purchasing this book about Granny Square motifs and how to join them. In this book we'll cover some basic stitches and techniques you'll need to start making Granny Squares. We'll also cover some popular methods for joining your motifs once you have crocheted them. I will also share some pretty border stitches you can use to give your projects a finishing touch.

This book is geared toward the beginner, so if you've never picked up a crochet hook and yarn you will be able to create beautiful Granny Square afghans, throws, and pillows once you finish this book. If you know how to crochet but want to learn different methods for joining your squares, then this book is also perfect for you. I'll take you step by step from square one to completing a project. So are you ready to create one of the enduring and popular types of crochet? Good, let's get started!

Yarn and Equipment Basics

Yarn comes in three basic fiber types: animal, plant, and synthetic. Animal fibers include wool, alpaca, cashmere, mohair, and angora. Plant fibers used for yarn include cotton, bamboo, hemp, and linen. Synthetic fibers used include acrylic, polyester, microfiber, and other types of petroleum based fibers. Most yarn is manufactured in the same manner. Fibers are processed, cleaned, and dyed. They are then spun into yarn and then spun into skeins, balls, or hanks. Yarn comes in weights ranging from fingerling (0) to super bulky (7).

As a beginner I would recommend choosing a medium weight acrylic yarn. Acrylic yarn is made from synthetic fibers so it is easy to care for and easy to work with. Acrylic yarn can be machine washed and dried and doesn't need any special care. It also holds it shape well and comes in a wide variety of colors.

You will need a selection of crochet hooks. You can find nice quality and inexpensive aluminum hooks in sets from E to K. These are the sizes you will use most when crocheting projects. You can also find crochet hooks in bamboo, wood, and plastic.

Clip on stitch markers are also handy tools to have. They are used to mark where a round begins and ends, pattern repeats, and color changes. A nice pair of scissors or shears used only for thread and yarn, a tote or bag to store your yarn and projects in, and a good light source are also needed to begin.

How to Understand a Yarn Label

When you go to buy yarn the first thing you want to look at is not only the color, but the yarn label. The yarn label will tell you many things you need to know to choose the correct yarn for your project. The following image is from a skein of Red Heart Super Save in Perfect Pink. The yarn is a medium weight (4) yarn made from acrylic fibers. A gauge swatch (a four inch by four inch swatch of crochet fabric) crocheted with a size US I/9 crochet hook will produce a swatch that will have 17 stitches in each row, and 23 rows. (Always make a gauge swatch before you work a pattern so you can see if you need to go up or down a hook size or if you need to tighten up or loosen up your tension.) The care symbols also indicate that you can machine wash and dry the fabric at no hotter than 104 degree.

You can find a complete list of care symbols which you can download and print out at Lion Brand Yarn. I've shared the link in the Resource section at the end of this book.

Choosing Your Yarn Colors

Some of the prettiest Granny square afghans are made from scraps of yarn leftover from crochet projects. Each square will be unique and your afghan will be very colorful. If you want to crochet a throw or afghan with a certain color palette then you will need to choose colors which go together or complement each other. One example of a color palette is to choose a main color, a secondary color, and a complimentary color. Complimentary colors are opposite colors on the color wheel. These include blue and orange, green and red, and yellow and purple. Neutral colors include white, ivory, gray, and black. Using black to join the squares creates a stunning stained glass window effect. Don't be shy about choosing your colors. If you like the color combinations go for it. This is your work of art and a way to express your creativity.

How Big Should You Make Your Afghan?

Now that you've decided on the color scheme how big should you make your afghan? Here's two handy charts to help you. The first table is a guide for the width of your project. The second table is a guide for the length of your project.

To translate this into how many squares you should make you will first need to know how big your squares will be. Granny squares can range from petite three inch squares to one large square. Most Granny squares are somewhere between six and 12 inches square. So if you are making six inch squares and you want to make a baby blanket you will need six squares to get a width of 36 inches, and you will need six squares to get a length of 36 inches. So to crochet a baby blanket using six inch squares you would need 36 squares in total because you would need six across and six in length. Six times six equals 36.

Another example would be for a twin bed with drape. Using six inch squares you would need 11 squares for the width and 15 in length. Take 11 multiplied by 15 and you will need 165 squares to create a twin size throw with drape over the sides of the bed.

For a simple rule of thumb take the number of squares you will need for the width and multiply it by the number of squares you will need for the length. This will give you the total number of squares you will need for your project.

WIDTH	
Size	Inches
Receiving Blanket	24 Inch
Stroller Blanket	30 Inch
Cradle Blanket	18 Inch
Baby Blanket	36 Inch
Twin Bed (Top of Mattress Only)	39 Inch
Twin Bed with Drape	66 Inch
Full/Double Bed (Top of Mattress Only)	54 Inch
Full Double Bed with Drape	80 Inch
Queen Bed (Top of Mattress Only)	60 Inch
Queen Bed with Drape	90 Inch
King Bed (Top of Mattress Only)	76 Inch
King Bed with Drape	108 Inc

LENGTH

Size	Inches
Receiving Blanket	24 Inch
Stroller Blanket	40 Inch
Cradle Blanket	36 Inch
Baby Blanket	36 Inch
Twin Bed (Top of Mattress Only)	75 Inch
Twin Bed with Drape	90 Inch
Full/Double Bed (Top of Mattress Only)	75 Inch
Full Double Bed with Drape	90 Inch
Queen Bed (Top of Mattress Only)	80 Inch
Queen Bed with Drape	100 Inc
King Bed (Top of Mattress Only)	80 Inch
King Bed with Drape	100 Inc

Basic Crochet Stitches

In this chapter we'll learn the basic crochet stitches you need to start and complete a Granny square afghan or throw. The stitches we'll cover include slip knot, chain stitch, slip stitch, single crochet, double crochet, and how to crochet in the round. Once you master these stitches you'll be ready to create your very own Granny square afghan or throw.

Slip Knot

The first step is to get the yarn onto your crochet hook. This is done by creating a slip knot and sliding it onto your hook. Gently snug the slip knot up so it's not too sloppy, but don't pull it up too tightly. It should move freely on your crochet hook.

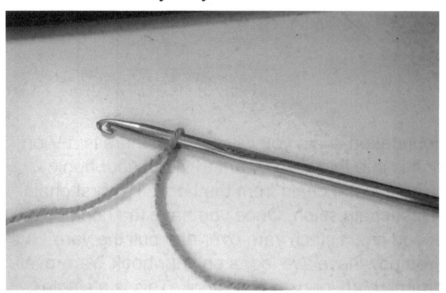

Chain Stitch

In order to start crocheting a Granny square you'll need a base of chain stitches. Hold the hook in your dominant hand (I'm right handed so all of the examples will show right handed crocheting) and hold the yarn in your other hand. Place the yarn over the hook and pull it through the slip knot. This is the first chain stitch. You never count the slip knot as a stitch.

Place the yarn over the hook again (known as a yarn over) and pull it through the first chain stitch. Now you have two chain stitches. Practice crocheting chain stitches until your chain is nice and even. All of your stitches should be the same size and tension. Don't worry if you have to practice a few times to get it right. Practice as much as you need and take your time.

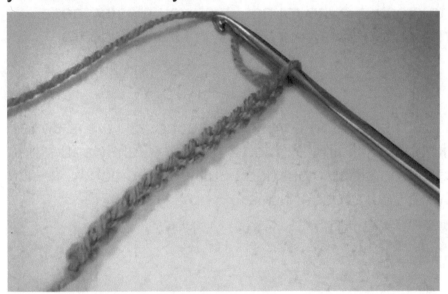

Single Crochet

If you look at your foundation chain you will see that there is a V on the top of the chain. It is into this V you want to insert your hook. Insert the hook into the second chain from the hook. The first chain stitch counts as the first chain stitch. Once you have the hook inserted into the second chain stitch yarn over and pull the yarn through the stitch. You now have two loops on your hook. Yarn over and pull the yarn through both loops on the hook. This is a single crochet stitch. Insert the hook into the next stitch, yarn over and pull through. Yarn over and pull through the two loops on the hook. Now you have three single crochet stitches since you count the first chain stitch as a single crochet and you have crocheted two chain stitches. Continue to crochet across the foundation chain ending in the last chain stitch.

If you were flat crocheting you would then turn your work, chain one and insert the hook into the second stitch from the hook to begin a new row. Each time you turn your work you will chain one for the first single crochet stitch and then insert the hook into the second stitch from the hook to start crocheting the row.

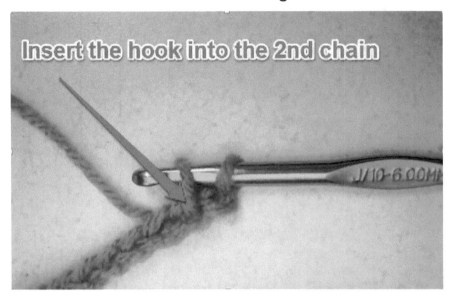

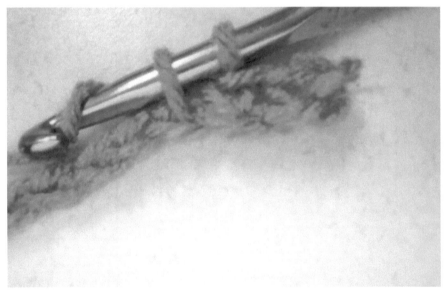

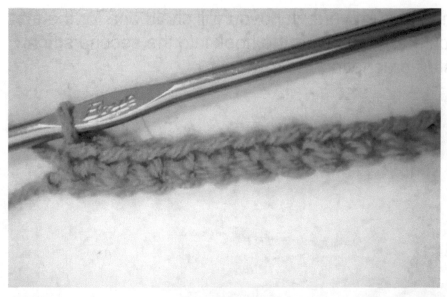

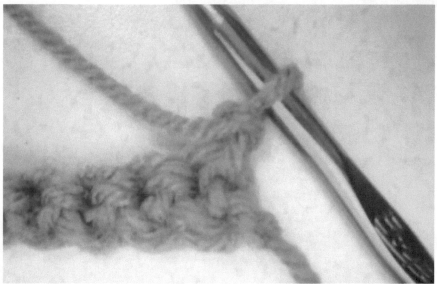

Double Crochet

The groups of stitches which are iconic of the Granny square are crocheted with double crochet stitches. Groups of double crochet are also called shells. To crochet a double crochet start at the beginning of a row and chain three (this is called the starting chain). This is counted as the first double crochet stitch. Yarn over and insert the hook into the second stitch from the hook (or fourth chain from the hook if you are starting a new project and using a foundation chain), yarn over and pull through the stitch. You will now have three loops on the hook. Yarn over and pull through the first two loops, yarn over and pull through the last two loops on the hook. To crochet the next stitch yarn over, insert the hook into the next stitch, pull through and yarn over and pull through the first two loops, yarn over and pull through the last two loops. Continue to the end of the row and work the last stitch into the last stitch of the row. Turn your work and chain three. When you work across the row crochet the last in the third chain of the starting chain, and then turn your work to begin a new row.

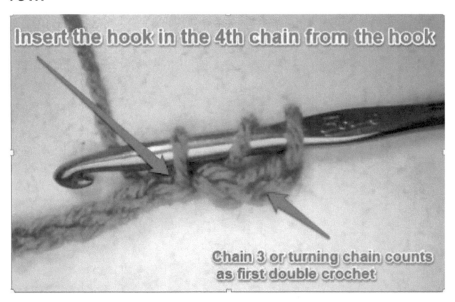

Insert the hook in the 4th chain from the hook

Chain 3 or turning chain counts as first double crochet

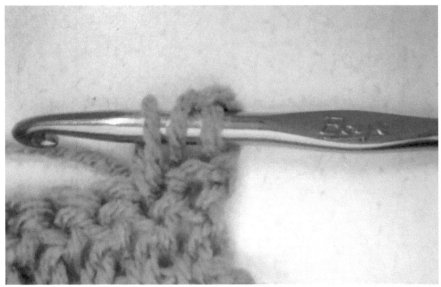

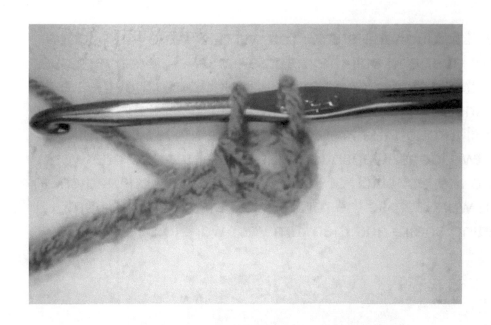

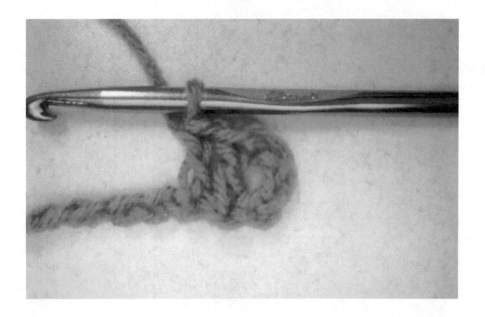

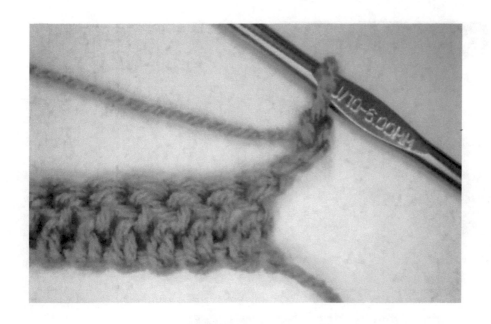

Working in the Round

When you are crocheting Granny squares and other motifs you will be crocheting in the round. Once you crochet the appropriate number of chain stitches insert the hook into the first chain stitch, yarn over and pull through the stitch and pull through the loop on the hook. This is a slip stitch. This joins the chain and enables you to work in the round. It is important to make sure the chain does not twist if you have several chain stitches you are joining. If the chain twists simply take the slip stitch out and rejoin the chain making sure it is not twisted.

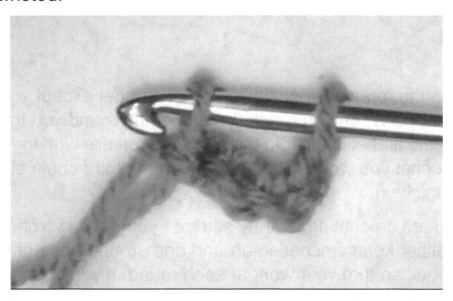

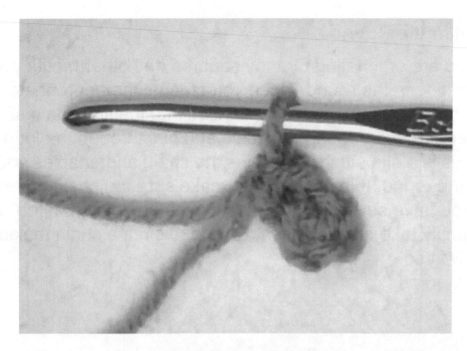

Working in the round is very similar to flat crochet except you rarely turn your work. When you reach the end of the round you the slip stitch into the first stitch to join the round. If you are working with double crochet you would join the round in the third chain stitch of the starting chain.

When you are crocheting Granny squares you have two choices. You can either keep crocheting around and around and not turn your work, or you can turn your work at each round. If you choose not to turn your work the inside of your square will naturally be a bit crooked. This is because of the tension of the yarn and the way the stitches come together. This is natural and very acceptable.

If you choose to turn your work after each round your Granny square will be straight and the center will not be crooked. This is also acceptable. It is a matter if personal choice on turning your work or not. Try each method and see which look you like the best. Here's an example of a giant Granny square I'm working on. I change colors at each round and have not turned my work. You can see how the center is a bit wonky, but I like it in this project. I think it gives it a bit of personality. The next time I do this throw I may turn my work and have a perfectly square project. We'll just have to see how my mood swings that day.

Creating a Granny Square

Now that we've learned about yarn and what equipment you need, and we've learned the basic stitches it's now time to start a Granny square. The first step is to create a starting chain. Chain three and join the chain in the first chain stitch with a slip stitch. Insert the hook into the first chain stitch, yarn over and pull through and then pull through the loop on your hook.

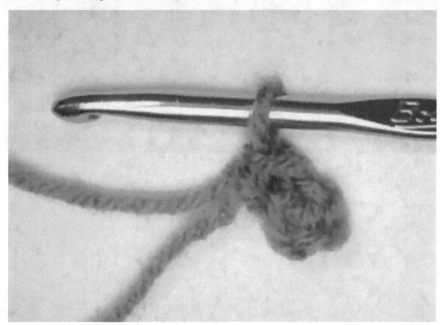

Round One

Now we're ready to crochet round one. Do not insert the hook into the stitches, but into the hole in the center of the circle. We will be making four sets of three double crochet separated by three chain stitches. Begin by chaining three. This counts and the first double crochet in the first cluster. Crochet two double crochet stitches into the circle in the middle of the joined foundation chain.

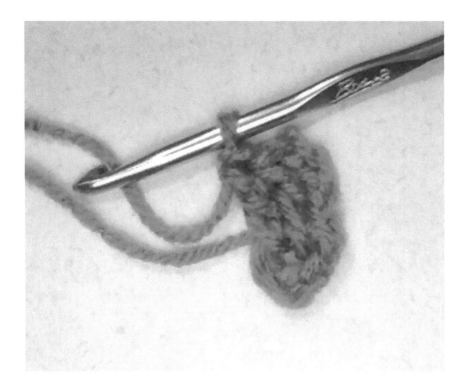

Chain three. The chain three sets will act as the corners for the next round. Crochet three double crochet again, chain three, three double crochet, chain three, three double crochet, and chain three. Join the round with a slip stitch into the third chain of the starting chain of the first cluster. If you are going to change colors pull up about six inches and cut the yarn. Then pull the tail through the fabric to the back of the square with the crochet hook.

If I were to write this pattern out it would look like this:

Ch 3, join

Rnd 1: Ch 3, 2 dc, *ch 3, 3 dc* work pattern rep 3 times, join

When you see * in a pattern it denotes the beginning of a pattern repeat. Repeat the instructions between the *'s the appropriate number of times.

If you are going to use the same color and not turn your work you will need to slip stitch into the next two double crochet stitches. Slip stitch into the chain three space and chain three to begin the first cluster of stitches. You can also turn your work and begin the first cluster in the chain three space if you wish to turn your work after each row if you are not changing colors.

To start a new color create a slip knot and place it on the hook. In any chain three space insert the hook and slip stitch around the chain three space to join the new color. Be sure to leave at least six inches of a tail for the new color to weave in at the end of the project. You can also weave the ends in as you go. This is what I do because I don't want to have to deal with a bunch of tails at the end of the project.

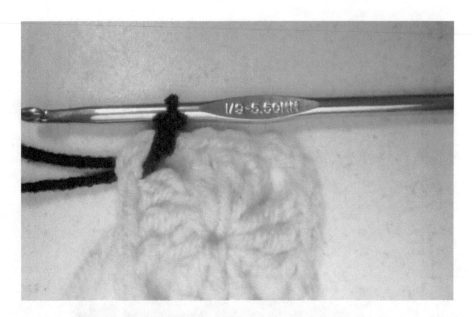

To start a new round chain three. Crochet two double crochet, chain three, three double crochet into the chain three space. Capture the tail of the yarn under the first three stitches like so:

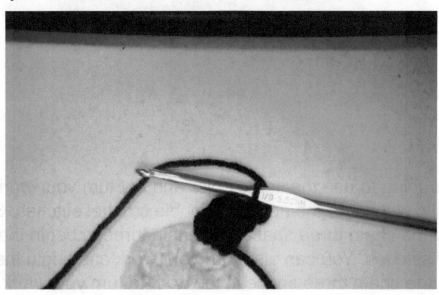

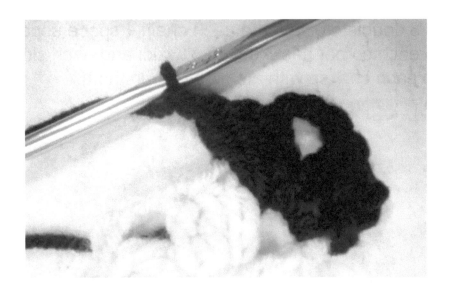

Now crochet three double crochet, chain three, three double crochet into the next chain three space and chain one. Repeat this twice more and join into the third chain stitch of the starting chain. Pull up at least six inches and cut the yarn. Pull the tail to the back of your work and attach the next color in any corner chain three space. Continue to work the Granny square in this manner until you have reached the desired size.

Here is a Granny square pattern written out:

Abbreviations: ch = chain, dc = double crochet, sp = space, Rnd = Round

Chain 3 and join

Rnd 1: Ch 3, 2 dc *ch 3, 3 dc* twice, join.

Rnd 2: Join new color in any ch 3 sp, Ch 3, 2 dc, ch 3, 3 dc, *ch 1, in ch 3 sp work 3 dc, ch 3, 3 dc* three times and join.

Rnd 3: Join new color in any ch 3 sp Ch 3, 2 dc, ch 3, 3 dc, *ch 1, 3 dc in ch 1 sp, ch 1, in ch 3 sp work 3 dc, ch 3, 3 dc* three times, join.

Rnd 4: Join new color in any ch 3 sp Ch 3, 2 dc, ch 3, 3 dc, ch 1, *3 dc in ch 1 sp twice, in ch 3 sp work 3 dc, ch 3, 3 dc*, work pattern repeat three times and join.

If you want your Granny square larger continue to work 3 double crochet, chain 3, 3 double crochet in each corner space (chain 3 space) and 3 double crochet into each chain 1 space separated by a chain 1. So each corner has 3 dc, ch 3, 3 dc; and each side has 3 dc worked into each ch 1 sp with a ch 1 between them.

Weaving in the Tails

In order for your squares not to unravel you will need to weave in the tails. Thread a tapestry needle with the tail and weave it in and out of the stitches, turn the square and weave the tail in and out of the stitches, turn the square and weave the tail in and out of the stitches again. If you weave the tail in and out of the square's stitches three times changing direction each time the tails will be secure and your square will not come undone.

Joining

Once you have all of your squared crocheted you have a few choices on how to join them. Each method has its benefits and gives your project a different look. In this chapter we'll learn how to use single crochet to create and edged framed look to your squares, slip stitch, and whip stitch joining methods.

Single Crochet

Hold two squares together with wrong sides together. Join the color you wish to use in any corner space. Insert the hook into the corner space catching both squares and slip stitch. Chain one. Insert the hook into the front and back square in the first double crochet stitch, yarn over and pull through. Yarn over and pull through the two loops on the hook.

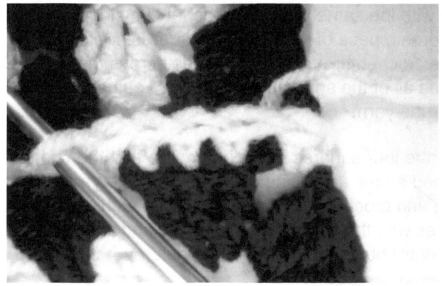

Continue with the same yarn and crochet two single crochet stitches into the corner space of the next two squares. Match up the stitches and single crochet through both squares across the edge. Once you have joined all of the squares you need to you can pull up a long tail and break the yarn.

Now take the four squares and fold them to that the wrong sides of the unjoined edges are facing upwards. Join the yarn in the corner, chain one and crochet one single crochet. Match up the stitches on the squares with the wrong sides together and single crochet across the edge until you reach the center corner.

Crochet one single crochet, slip stitch into the single crochet chain of the first joining and single crochet into the next corner. Match up the squares and single crochet across to the next corner and repeat if you have more squares to join. If not pull up a long tail and break the yarn.

Join all of the squares in this manner. I find it easier to join the squares in rows and then join the row. You can join rows as you go or wait until you have all of your squares crocheted and then join them. I usually wait until I have all of the Granny squares crocheted and then start to join them, but it is your own choice.

As you can see the single crochet join creates a pretty framed effect. If you don't want the raised stitches on the right side then you can join your squares by holding the right sides together. I used a contrasting color so you could see the stitches, but you can use the same color as the last round for a less prominent effect.

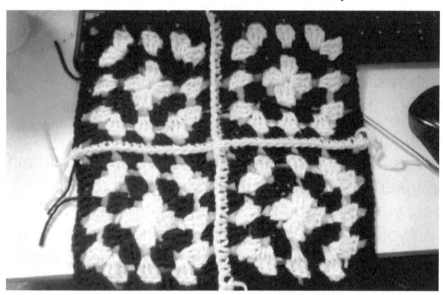

Front

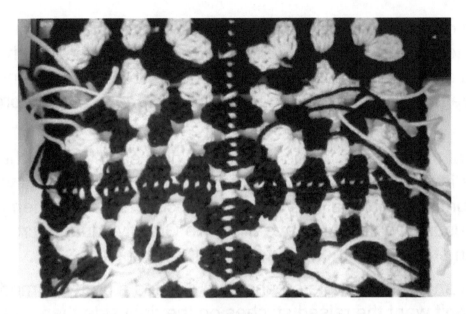

Back

Slip Stitch Join

Another easy way to join your Granny squares is to use a slip stitch. A slip stitch differs from a single crochet because you don't yarn over once you pull the yarn through the stitch, but you pull the loop through the loop already on your hook. A slip stitch join also gives you a bit of a ridge, but not one as prominent as single crochet.

Begin by placing a slip knot on your hook. Insert the hook into any corner space and create a slip stitch to join the yarn. Slip stitch again in the corner space. Insert the hook into the first double crochet stitch of both squares, yarn over and pull all the way through the stitch and the loop on your hook. Slip stitch into the next two double crochet stitches and crochet one slip stitch in the chain one space. Continue across the square and when you come to the corner space slip stitch twice, pick up the next two squares and slip stitch twice into the corner space and work your way across the square. When you get all of the squares joined pull the yarn up and leave at least six inches to weave in and cut the yarn.

Be sure to catch both loops of the double crochet stitch for both squares in the slip stitch.

Slip stitch on the right side done in navy. You can see how it forms a small ridge which can be very attractive to frame the squares. In the next two images you can see how it looks when the slip stitch is done in white. In my opinion it is not as attractive as a single crochet join in white, but if you like it that is all that matters.

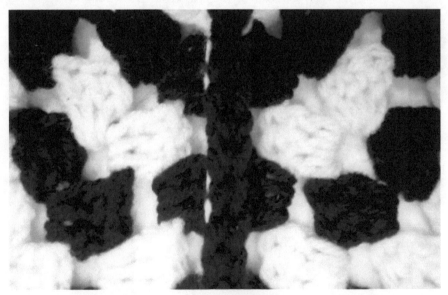

Slip stitch on right side done in white

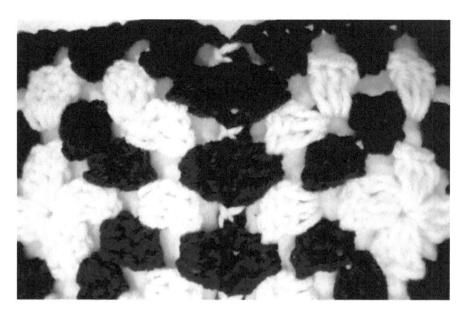

Slip stitch done in white wrong side

Whip Stitch Join

The whip stitch join is perhaps the easiest join to use. Thread a tapestry or blunt yarn needle with yarn and whip stitch the squares together. In the corners catch one loop of each chain on each square. I use two whip stitches in the corners to really secure them and keep the squares square. Catch both loops of the double crochet stitches on each square keeping the stitches aligned. When you come to a chain one space catch one loop of each square in the whip stitch. If you use a coordinating color to whip stitch your squares together you will have an almost invisible seam with no ridge.

Catch both loops of the stitches in the whip stitch.

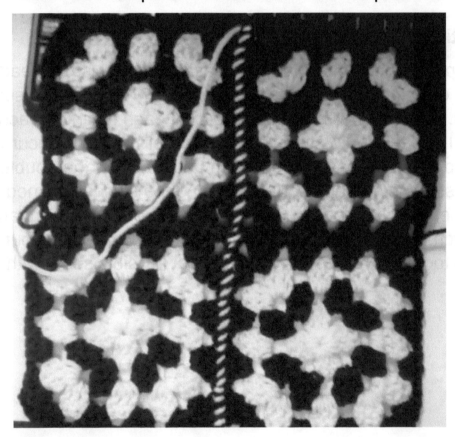

In this image you can see how the navy seam is almost invisible while the white seam is very apparent.

Which method you use is a matter of personal preference and the effect you wish your project to have. A pretty contrasting yarn used with the single crochet join can form a frame for each square. You can have this ridge on the right or the wrong side of your project. I would recommend using a coordinating yarn with the slip stitch and whip stitch join to create an almost invisible join. While the slip stitch will give you a bit of a ridge the stitches are not as defined as in a single crochet join. Be sure to check out the video links I've included in the Resource section about different methods to join your squares.

Edging Stitches and Techniques

Okay so you've got your squares crochet and joined. I can imagine your project is very pretty, but an edging will give it a finished look and add even more beauty. My first tip on edging is to work at least one row of single crochet all of the way around your afghan or throw. This gives you a nice even base to crochet an edging.

Join the yarn in any corner, chain one and single crochet two stitches. Crochet a single crochet into each double crochet and one in each chain one space. When you get to where the squares are joined crochet two single crochet into the first corner space, pull the joining yarn to the back of your work and slip stich into the joining chain, and then single crochet two stitches into the next corner space. You can then work your way across the square working a single crochet into each double crochet and chain one space. At the corners of your afghan or throw crochet three single crochet into the corner spaces.

When you come back around to the beginning of the border slip stitch into the chain one. If you are going to use the same yarn to do the edging you don't have to cut the yarn. But if you're going to change colors be sure to pull up at least six inches before you cut the yarn so you can weave in the tails securely.

You can leave this as the border or do another round of single crochet in the other color or contrasting color.

There are many different types of edging and border you can crochet to add a finishing embellishment to your project. Here are a few of my favorites that any beginner can crochet.

Simple Chain Edging

Join the yarn in any stitch, chain 3, skip one stitch, single crochet. Continue to chain three, skip one stitch and single crochet all of the way around the afghan or throw. Join in the beginning chain stitch.

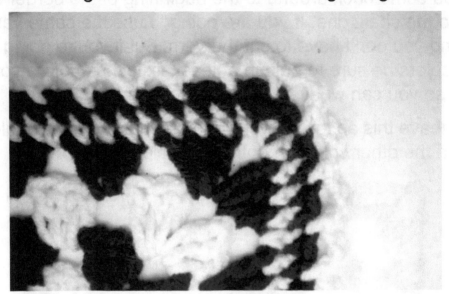

Simple Shell Edging

Another very simple but pretty edging is a simple shell stitch. Join the yarn in any stitch and chain 3. Double crochet 2 more stitches in the same space and skip one stitch. Three double crochet in the next stitch, skip a stitch, three double crochet in the next stitch all of the way around the afghan or throw. At the corners crochet a shell, single crochet and then another shell.

Ruffled Shell Edging

Join the yarn in any stitch. Chain three and skip a stitch, single crochet. Chain three and skip a stitch and single crochet all of the way around the afghan or throw. You can then turn your work and work the shells on the wrong side, but if you break the yarn and then join the yarn in any chain three space your shells will be much prettier on the right side.

Join the yarn and chain three. Crochet two double crochet into the chain three space, slip stitch into the single crochet stitch. Crochet three double crochet into each chain three space and slip stitch into the single crochet between each shell.

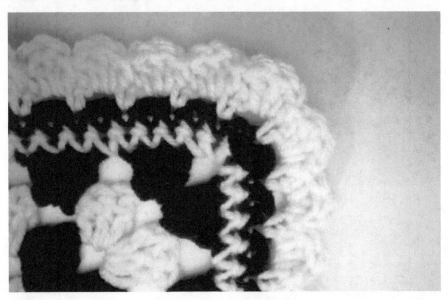

End Notes

Thank you so much for purchasing this book on how to create a Granny square afghan or throw. Granny squares are a classic motif used for many projects. Not only can you create heirloom afghans but you can also crochet cute bags and unique garments using Granny squares. It is my hope that this book has helped you to gain the confidence and skills to tackle a large project. Don't be afraid to experiment with colors and try out new combinations and styles of squares. The main thing is to have fun and let your creativity flow,

All my best,

Dorothy

Filet Crochet

Learn the Timeless Art of Filet Crochet

By Dorothy Wilks

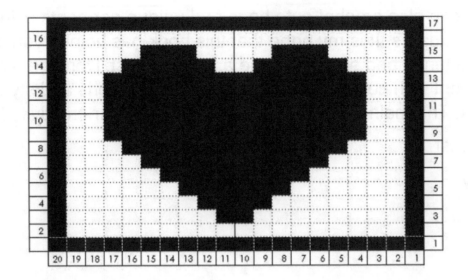

Thank you for purchasing this book on Filet crochet. Filet crochet is an art form which made a resurgence in popularity lately. One of the reasons is because Filet crochet is a beautiful way to create timeless heirlooms. If you know how to crochet a chain stitch, single crochet, and double crochet you already have the skills you need to learn Filet crochet. In this book we'll learn the basics of the Filet crochet techniques, how to crochet the stitches used, and how to read a graph pattern for Filet. I will also share with you some easy Filet chart patterns for you to practice your new skills. Ready? Let's get started!

Contents

Reading a Filet Graph

Filet crochet uses graphs instead of written patterns. A graph gives you a visual representation of the pattern. I know you may be nervous about trying to read a graph, but really it's quite easy once you understand the structure of a graph and how it is crocheted.

Graph Basics

Here is an example of a blank graph. You will notice right off the row numbers are on each side of the graph. This is to make it easier to keep track of which row you are working on, and because the odd rows are worked from right to left and the even rows are worked from left to right. You will also notice the graph has darker lines every 10 squares and every 10 rows. This is to also help you to keep track of where you are in the pattern.

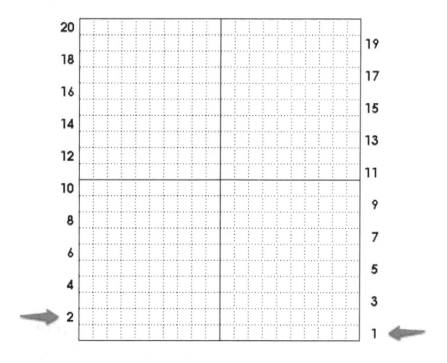

This example shows a very simple Filet pattern. The gray squares indicate solid squares and the white squares indicate open squares. You always start in the lower right hand corner and work from right to left. So the first row is 20 filled in squares. For the next row you move up to Row 2 and work from left to right. This means you crochet 1 filled in square, 8 open squares, 2 filled in squares, 8 open squares, and end with 1 filled in square. Row 3 is read from right to left, and so on up to the last row of the pattern.

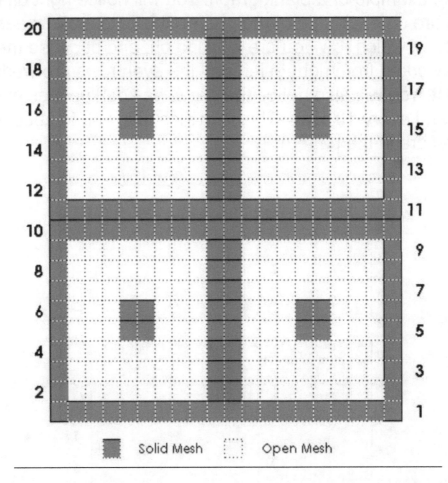

Solid Mesh   Open Mesh

As you work up the graph make a mark on the pattern or use sticky notes to show which way you are working. When you change rows flip the sticky note and place it on the appropriate row. Graphs are that simple.

Basics of the Filet Crochet Technique

Each square in a Filet chart represent either 2 or 3 stitches. Personally I prefer to use 3 stitches per square because I feel this gives a better defined pattern. In the following chart there are 10 squares across a row. If we use 3 stitches per square our foundation chain needs to be 30 stitches. A simple formula to remember this is to take the number of squares in the chart and multiply them by three. This will give you the correct number of foundation stitches.

Most Filet patterns use double crochet stitches. So you will need to add 2 to the foundation chain for the first double crochet in the row. For the following chart crochet 30 chain stitches and then 2 more. Begin by crocheting the first double crochet into the 4th chain from the hook. Crochet double crochet stitches across the row since the first row is all solid mesh stitches.

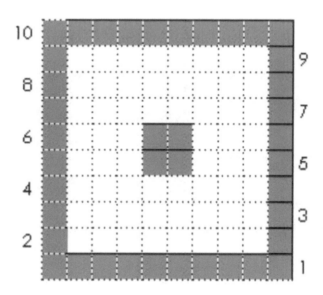

Solid Mesh

The grayed out squares represent solid mesh. The solid mesh Filet stitch is 3 double crochet stitches. Each time you see a solid square in a Filet graph you will do 3 double crochet stitches.

Chain and 2 double crochet for the 1st square

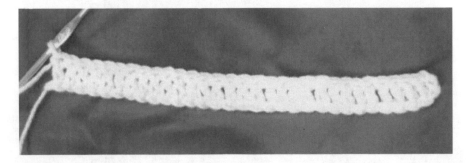

30 double crochet for the first row of 10 squares (3 sts per square)

Open Mesh

The white squares in the previous graph represent open mesh. The open mesh is crocheted with 1 double crochet and 2 chain stitches. For example in the second row first chain 3 and crochet 2 double crochet for the first square. The next square starts with a double crochet, chain 2, skip 2 stitches for the next square.

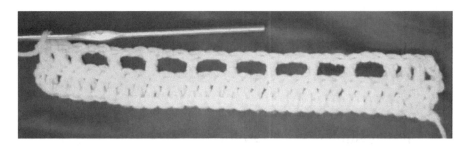

Row 3 starts with chain 3 for the first double crochet, 2 more double crochet for the first square. Now the double crochet stitches line up one on top of each other so for this row the open mesh starts with chain 2, skip 2 stitches, double crochet in the next stitch. Work across the row ending with 3 double crochet for the last square. You'll have 4 double crochet because of the way the mesh stitches and solid mesh stitches meet.

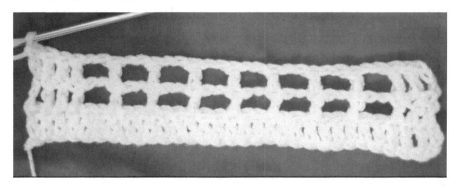

Lacet Stitch

The lacet stitch form pretty lace like patterns in the Filet fabric. The lacet stitch takes up 2 squares to crochet. Double crochet, chain3, skip 2 stitches, single crochet into the next stitch, chain three, skip 2 stitches, and begin the next square of stitches.

A lacet stitch on a graph is indicated with a V or a similar symbol. Check the key to the graph before you begin so you know what all of the symbols the designer used stand for.

Rectangles

After a row of lacet stitches you will need to close the top space so you can continue to crochet in the pattern. This is where rectangle stitches come in. These are 6 chain stitches, skip 6 stitches, and then double crochet into the next stitch. Or if you're going across the row the other way then you would start with a double crochet, chain 6, skip 6 stitches and then continue on with the next square. Rectangles normally are worked on top of lacet stitches so if the graph does not denote this then you know automatically to crochet rectangle stitches. Remember to line up the double crochet stitches of the active row with the previous row.

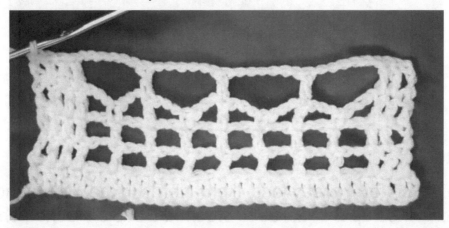

You can also use rectangles almost anywhere in a Filet pattern. They will usually be specified by two squares joined together on the graph. Once again be sure to check the key for the graph before you begin to crochet.

If the next row is open mesh the double crochet stitch of the second open mesh stitch is placed in the middle of the chain stitches of the rectangle.

Big Squares

Another variation of the Filet stitch is the big square. These are used to add space in a pattern. Big squares are flanked on both sides by solid mesh stitches. The big square takes two rows to complete. On the first row chain 9, skip 5 stitches, and double crochet. On the next row coming back across crochet a single crochet into the 2nd chain or the previous row, 6 single crochet around the next 6 chain stitches, and then 3 double crochet.

To finish the graph crochet a row of closed mesh stitches. If this pattern were written out it would take several lines, but with a graph you know exactly what to crochet and you can use graphs from designers who do not speak your native tongue.

Here is what the graph looks like for the piece of Filet crochet we just did.

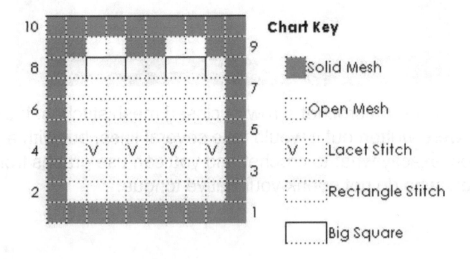

Now if I were write out the pattern it would look like this:

Chain 33

Row 1: dc in 4th ch from hook, dc into each st across, turn

Row 2: ch3, dc in each of the next 2 sts, *ch2, skv2 sts, dc into next st*repeat 7 times, 3dc into each of the next 3 sts, turn

Row 3: ch3, dc into each of the next 2 sts, *dc, ch2, skv2 sts* repeat 7 times, 3dc into each of the next 3 sts, turn

Row 4: ch3, dc into each of the next 2 sts, *dc, ch3, sk 2 sts, sc in next st, ch3, sk 2 sts* repeat 3 times, dc into each of the next 3 sts, turn

Row 5: ch3, dc into each of the next 2 sts, *ch6, dc into next dc of previous row* repeat 3 times, dc into each of the next 3 sts, turn

Row 6: ch3, dc in each of the next 2 sts, *ch2, skv2 sts, dc into next st*repeat 7 times, 3dc into each of the next 3 sts, turn

Row 7: ch3, dc into each of the next 5 sts, ch9, sk 5 sts, dc into each of the next 7 sts, ch9, sk 5 sts, dc into each of the next 7 sts, turn

Row 8: ch3, dc into each of the next 6 sts, sc into 2nd ch st, 6sc around ch6, dc into each of the next 5 sts, sc into 2nd ch st, 6sc around ch6, dc into each of the next 5 sts, turn

Row 9: ch3, dc into each st across, fasten off.

This is just for a small project; imagine how long the written instructions would be for a larger project. Graphs make it easy to see what the project will look like, and you can work them no matter what language you read or speak.

Easy Filet Patterns

Here are some simple Filet crochet patterns for you to practice your skills. You may even want to use a piece of graph paper and a pencil and design your own patterns. You can also use a program like Microsoft Excel like I did to design these patterns. For all of these charts I used the following symbols:

Closed Mesh

Open Mesh

V Lacet Stitch

Rectangle Stitch

Big Square

Filet Dishcloth

I used Lily Sugar 'n Cream cotton yarn in Peace and a size US G/6 (4.25mm) crochet hook for this pattern. If you want you could crochet a few rounds of single crochet around the dishcloth to finish it off.

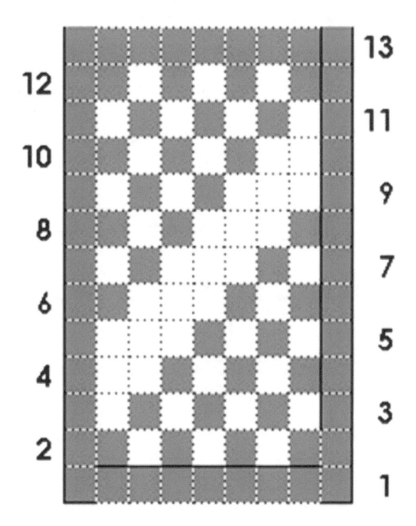

Filet Dresser Scarf

This pattern can be made as long as you like. Simply repeat the pattern until you reach the desired length of the scarf. To repeat the pattern repeat Rows 2-18 and end with Row 19 as the very last row. I used Lily Sugar 'n Cream Yarn in Light Blue and a US G/6 (4.25mm) crochet hook for this sample.

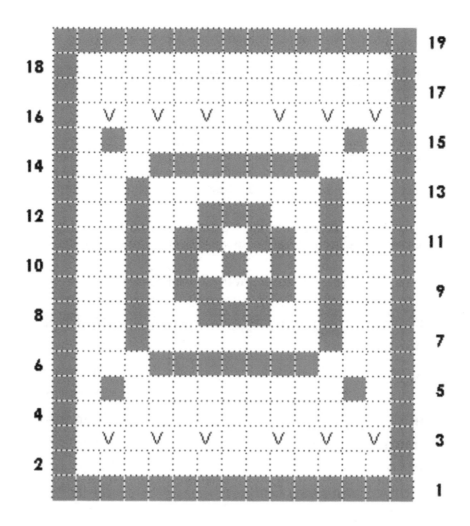

Filet Afghan Squares

Crochet these cute squares and join them together to create a lovely afghan for yourself or as a gift. You can use almost any type of yarn for Filet. I would not use a bulky yarn but weights from fingerling to worsted and medium weight yarn works well. You could also make these squares and whip stitch them together and make a unique scarf. There are many projects these squares lend themselves to, let your imagination be your guide.

Here is a handy chart for you to use to figure out how many squares you will need. For example if your squares measure 6 inches, then for a receiving blanket you would need 16 squares in total. That would be 4 squares across and 4 squares in length. Take these numbers and multiply them together and you get the total number of squares you need. If you want to make a twin for the top of the mattress only and your squares are 4 inches, you will need about 10 across for the width, and about 19 for the length. So 10 times 19 equal 190 squares in total.

I would crochet a round of single crochet or double crochet around the squares to give you a nice even round to join the squares. Do 3 stitches in each corner and evenly space the stitches up and down the sides.

I crocheted the samples using Red Heart Super Saver yarn and a size US G/6 (4.25mm) crochet hook.

Type of Afghan	Width	Lengt
Receiving Blanket	24 inches	24 inch
Stroller Blanket	30 inches	40 inch
Cradle	18 inches	36 inch
Baby Blanket	36 inches	36 inch
Twin Top of Mattress Only	39 inches	75 inch
Twin with Drape	66 inches	75 inch
Full/Double Top of Mattress Only	54 inches	75 inch
Full/Double with Drape	80 inches	90 inch
Queen Top of Mattress Only	60 inches	100 inc
Queen with Drape	90 inches	100 inc
King Top of Mattress Only	76 inches	80 inch
King with Drape	108 inches	100 inc

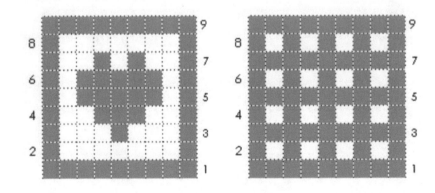

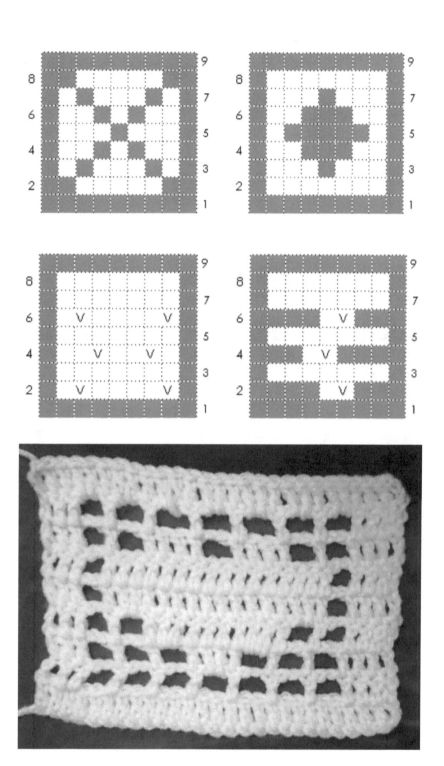

Cotton Coasters

Crochet a set of these up in no time to protect your surfaces from moisture. I used Lily Sugar 'n Cream cotton yarn in Coral Breeze Ombre and a size US G/6 (4.25mm) crochet hook for this example.

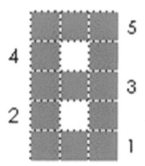

Edging
Row 1: Starting at a corner ch1, 2sc into same sp, sc evenly across each side and 3dc into each corner, turn
Row 2: *ch3, sk 1 st, sc* sl st into 1st ch st, fasten off and weave in tails.

End Notes

Thank you again for purchasing this book. I hope you enjoy learning Filet crochet and using the original designs I shared with you to practice your new skills. You can use almost any type of yarn for Filet crochet except bulky yarn. You can even use crochet thread to create very delicate projects. Although Filet crochet is traditionally done in white or ecru, don't be afraid to use any color you like. You can find lots of patterns on line especially on Pinterest. I've enjoyed writing this book, and I hope I have started you on a long journey of enjoyment with Filet crochet.

All my best,

Resources

Yarn Symbol Chart
http://www.lionbrand.com/yarnCare.html
Lion Brand Yarn

A Complete Library of How to Crochet Videos
https://www.youtube.com/playlist?list=PL7E4505A2C54EA604
The Crochet Crowd

Crochet for beginners : Easy traditional granny square

https://www.youtube.com/watch?v=0g1ylNMJQyl
NavyLouise

How To Attach Granny Squares - Method 1 Single Crochet
https://www.youtube.com/watch?v=DUe7rGpHXhc
The Crochet Crowd

How to Slip Stitch Crochet Squares Together Crochet Geek
https://www.youtube.com/watch?v=8WH8Lb4_qts
Crochet Geek

How To Attach Granny Squares - Method 3 - Sewing Together
https://www.youtube.com/watch?v=sGsuTctWK18
The Crochet Crowd

Made in United States
Troutdale, OR
01/02/2024

16648074R00038